outer edges

Other Books by Larry Kimmel

Blue Night
&
the inadequacy of long-stemmed roses

this hunger, tissue-thin

shards and dust

outer edges
a collection of tanka

Larry Kimmel

———

Stark Mountain Press
Colrain, MA

outer edges
a collection of tanka
1st edition

Stark Mountain Press
364 Wilson Hill Road
Colrain, MA 01340

http://starkmountainpress.tripod.com

ISBN: 978-0-9864328-0-4

Acknowledgments are due the editors of the following publications where these poems, sometimes in different form, first appeared: All the Shells: TSA Members' Anthology 2014; bottle rockets; Concise Delight; Bright Stars; Eucalypt; Modern English Tanka; MOONGARLIC; NeverEnding Story; Ribbons; Simply Haiku; Tanka Café; Two Milkweed Parachutes: TSA Newsletter.

Cover Photo by Kathleen Leahy
Cover Design by Larry Kimmel

Special thanks to

Linda Jeannette Ward
&
Stanford M. Forrester

– first friends of *outer edges* –

And the sizzling sheets of the town cried, Quick!-
Dylan Thomas

Dead men ...
They shall have stars at elbow and foot;
Dylan Thomas

Introduction

In the decade following his tanka collection *this hunger, tissue-thin*, Larry Kimmel has shown an unwavering course that always steers us to the outer edges--the appropriate title of his new collection of tanka.

> on the literary map,
> look for me
> at the outer edges
> where it reads
> *Here be Unicorns*

Kimmel is a poet who deftly ties evolutionary images to imagistic reflections of present reality, yet is grounded in family history and traditions. Here is a writer who can venture forth to a land of unicorns and dragons with a continuity that carries with it a love of heritage as expressed his 2007 prose poem *The Johnstown Flood* (Swamp Press), based on his maternal grandmother's account of her survival of that disaster in 1889.

Kimmel describes his approach to writing as "highly intuitive," based on "memories, imagination, desire."

He smoothly juxtaposes his enduring ties to family with sensory images that are among the best being written in modern English-language tanka:

hands that held
this family Bible held reins,
spun wool, penned
on yellowed fly-leaves
these brown and faded names

the sound of the siren
is as red
as your lips closing over
the blind white
of the hard boiled egg

Join me, then, in being transported along with the poet into viewing a Monet painting of Rouen in a steamy café window, and learn how one can use the tools of this world to transcend it.

espresso
by a steamed window
– Monet.
yes, Federal Street
could be Rouen in fog

horsehair, catgut
& rosin
how we use
this world
to transcend it

Complimenting Kimmel's blend of classic and imagistic, edgy tanka are two short sequences. My favorite is one he titles "monologes with tome-tombed men". Here he excels in the tanka practice of literary allusion combined with a form of direct address. Yet there is no mistaking this poet's tie to the modern world of Kindles, computers and digital photography.

> Issa,
> where have I gone wrong?
>   indifferent to housework
>   kindly to insects,
> but revered ? not at all

Linda Jeannette Ward
Coinjock, N.C.
April, 2015

outer edges

on my back
on a bed
in a bed & breakfast –
my dime destiny
mapped on a cracked ceiling

trying trying
to get hold of – not the hat,
wind-tumbled down the street,
but
my last earthly desire

to sculpt a destiny
or simply squeeze
the clay
and take what comes
?

this September day,
walking past the open windows
of a Tudor house
a sprinkle of arpeggios . . .
something long since lost

a jukebox femme
of the fifties still breathes
in the mind's ear –
all the woman I'd want to be
if woman I were

at the gallery entrance
she pauses
all hip & lipstick –
a nail driven through
a calendar date

on the literary map,
look for me
at the outer edges
where it reads
Here be Unicorns

the sound of the siren
is as red
as your lips closing over
the blind white
of the hard boiled egg

and I quote:
"nothing too good for the little lady –
clean t-shirt,
burgers at Wendy's,
bowling later"

in the streetlight
the red of her paisley dress purples
as do her lips –
lips that are saying
something that makes me blue

at the intersection
under a streetlit maple
emerald to amber to ruby
gems
of an accident

the mannequin's skirt flaps open
& open & o' how
this spring breeze taunts
recalling the quick nuptials
of amber afternoons & neon nights

looking down
on Central Street from the 28th floor,
toy-sized people –
and you in Provence,
a fading mini-fiction

in my mind's eye
I can see her in a thong &—& nothing . . .
my god!
so this is the life of the mind
who'd have thought

                    at the checkout
                    reading all
                    the tabloid headlines –
                    the curse
                    of literacy

talking with three guys
the co-ed shields herself
with a book –
                    imagine,
Shelley guarding her chastity

inside the grape arbor,
shadowed-patterns where her blouse
lies open –
the purple fruit
wants tasted

still water
crossed by a strict line on which sits
one bird
sharp as a glass negative
– no need to look up

his hand
at the moment of birth
a leaflet
his fate, his character
a decisive ideogram

hands that held
this family Bible held reins,
spun wool, penned,
on yellowed fly-leaves,
these brown and faded names

no one left
to tell again the family stories,
the farm stories,
and how the great poet came to sit
in the chair I sit in now

gas flames rise
from fake logs,

the tribe's
story teller,

a Kindle

while I wait
to be served, I devise a story
in the willowware –
we've each of us our beliefs
and our own supporting evidence

that we can live on finer
& finer energy fields –
sure, why not?
if you can believe this world
you can believe any world

October.
on my way to Bar Harbor
stuttering tree shadows
trouble my brain
like a strobe

espresso
by a steamed window
– Monet.
yes, Federal Street
could be Rouen in fog

Dec. 24th - 25th

falling snow
past streetlights holiday
the parking lot –
at Starbucks an answer
from tomorrow's Toyko

wide snow,
all else perpendicular – the tall trees,
the icicles off the porch eve –
    and I, too, am upright
    in my solitude

        by lantern light
        stacking pennies
        five deep
        & five deep –
        waiting out the storm

Nefertiti –
was there ever such a woman?
what I wouldn't give
to stand in her aura,
know what she thought of her world

in wet sand
the chain
of her elegant footsteps
end
midway to nowhere

always fascinated by
that last half-inch in the long crawl
of evolution
where mankind straightens
to step out of the picture

eons ago
an Eocene fish got buried in mud –
now framed
on my stairway wall
its fossiled fame

the sizzle
of crickets
tightens –
something about this mountain night
remembers ancient seas

glint
of braceleted arms, body
maddered by firelight –
I wake! to a trace
of goat and sandalwood

I step out
on the patio for breakfast –
hey, maybe my neighbor's right,
why listen to bird song
when you can rev an engine?

noontime
and already I'm 2 dvd.s
wiser
and 4 cups of espresso
stronger

all at once,
the abuse of a decade
condensed into a bullet –
    there's a house for sale
    in our neighborhood

glimpsed
through the blind sockets
of the skull
that hollow
where the live brain lived

dusk
and the day lily all but done
    no one
    a statistic
    but once

horsehair, catgut
& rosin –
how we use
this world
to transcend it

I conjure our river bank
but it morphs,
it jungles
and the Rousseau-animals emerge –
those eyes! our sudden nakedness!

the sea-green pool
in the woodland river –
after 30 years and all
the great capitals of the world,
the sea-green pool

lying
under stars
becoming
a wide slow
river

waking to the fact of morning

bird peepings at first light
   I wake (fetal)
   wishing I hadn't
unanswered emails
       nag

     haiku
     happening . . . must
         r e a c h
     bedside
     pen . . .

coffee to brew. this dailiness –
  keep
  moving keep-keep moving keep
  – rosebuds o p e n i n g
in dew time

                    door wide on
                    weather mostly sunny
                                &
                                mild
                    with chances . . .

          we've come through
          again
          sunlight crosscuts the kitchen
          motes circling – light   shade   light
                              cosmos in small

                              coffee mug in hand
                    the routine of bee & clover
                                    – yes!
                    "all's right with the world"
                                – and now the news

                    _____

**monologues
with tome-tombed men**

1
hang it all Browning,
it could almost be mine,
your *Andrea del Sarto.*[1]
his impossible love
and the greats known by him

[1] a paraphrase from A Draft of XXX Cantos; II,
by Erza Pound

2
Langland,[2]
when writing your great Vision
in Chaucer's London
you could not have envisioned this –
your words on my monitor tonight

    — 2a
though six centuries sundered,
I find us fused by a common guilt
    verse
    vs.
    wage-work

    — 2b
quoting, you wrote
"the laborer is worth his hire"
tell me about it! –
    still, my needs are met
    and my wants somewhat

[2] William Langland, 14th century author of
The Vision of Piers Plowman

3
and you, the sage of Concord [3]
    sane, credible, astute –
a common man
wild
in your own quiet way

   — 3a
   mornings you wrote
   afternoons hoed
   took late walks to the Pond –yes,
   but those lamplit conversations . . . o,
   to have been a fly on your wall

   — 3b
   trust thyself – your message
   or as Campbell phrased it,
   follow your bliss –
   well I have,
   guilt and lies not withstanding

[3] Ralph Waldo Emerson

4
Han Shan,[4] like you,
I never thought it'd end this way –
    you 'neath your pine
    me, my sumac,
our red dust days gone with the wind

5
Issa,[5]
where have I gone wrong? –
    indifferent to housework
    kindly to insects,
but revered –?   not at all

postscript:

not surprising, is it?, that more
and more, as each old friend ends
his or her grave march,
I hold endless monologues
with tome-tombed men

———————

[4] 9th century Chinese Taoist poet, aka 'Cold Mountain'
[5] Kobayashi Issa, one of the four Japanese haiku masters

About the Author

Larry Kimmel was born in Johnstown, PA. He holds degrees from Oberlin Conservatory and Pittsburgh University, and has worked at everything from steel mills to libraries. Now self-employed, he lives with his wife in the hills of western Massachusetts.

To learn more about the work of Larry Kimmel
see:
http://larrykimmel.tripod.com